Advance praise for
Teacher/Pizza Guy

"I never really cared for poetry, but I truly loved Kass's work. He speaks to all of our insecurities and vulnerabilities, giving a voice to what we want to say but rarely do. Yes, teachers are struggling to get by financially, and it's a shame that education is not being made a higher priority in our society. Thank you, Jeff, for opening the door to this conversation in a creative and enriching way."

—David Hecker, president of AFT Michigan

"After twenty-plus years of teaching, I can say that these poems capture more of a teacher's life than any news story, assigned manual, or documentary account ever could. To read them is to experience the inspiring, infuriating, hilarious, tedious, and quietly glorious lives lived by one teacher residing in the twenty-first century as a fully realized and flawed human being. They will speak to your heart and mind regardless of which side of the big desk you've ever been on."

—Sean Sabo, teacher, Ann Arbor, Michigan

"Kass's hip-hop poetic style illuminates the gritty yet inspiring realities of teaching today's youth, while at the same time working a second job to make ends meet. *Teacher/Pizza Guy* will resonate with those who have ever strived to make a difference, no matter with kids by day, pizzas at night, or both. Kass is a distinctive poet with insight and compassion who ultimately 'chooses bliss.'"

—Don Packard, English department chairperson,
Ann Arbor Pioneer High School

"Here we have poems of labor, wages, busted knees, and the miracles of bodies at all. Forged out of economic precarity and the ways that such uncertainty shapes a life (its breaths, hours, delights, resistance), Kass's poems strain toward what is broken, depleted, or overlooked, and find song there. These are not songs of repair, but songs that praise and document some of the effortful lasting, and attempts to last, of Kass's most beloved subjects. In this way these poems carry the intimacy and goodbye of an elegy, the attentiveness of the ode, and the urgency of the protest cry."

—Aracelis Girmay, author of *The Black Maria*

"What a beautiful and moving and funny and un-heroic and angry and tender and honest book of poems about labor, aging, love, and, as Kass says, finding 'meaning in every ice patch on the sidewalk.' This book's heart is enormous. I love it."

—Ross Gay, author of *Catalog of Unabashed Gratitude* and *The Book of Delights*

"Jeff Kass affirms the dignity and heartbreak of the working person with funny and deeply human turns and terms. A master storyteller, Kass reminds us in *Teacher/Pizza Guy* of the elasticity and liminality we negotiate in our relationships between teacher and student, working and working poor, life and death. Kass is in the middle of the country, a humble Hercules, trying to pull it all together with grace, beauty, and a touching humility. He will make you cry and laugh and remember to hold your head high and hope."

—Kevin Coval, author of *A People's History of Chicago* and *Everything Must Go: The Life & Death of an American Neighborhood*

TEACHER/
PIZZA GUY

Made in Michigan Writers Series

General Editors

Michael Delp, Interlochen Center for the Arts
M. L. Liebler, Wayne State University

A complete listing of the books in this series can be found online
at wsupress.wayne.edu

TEACHER/
PIZZA GUY

POEMS BY
JEFF KASS

WAYNE STATE UNIVERSITY PRESS
DETROIT

ISBN 978-0-8143-4715-7 (paperback)
ISBN 978-0-8143-4716-4 (e-book)

Library of Congress Control Number: 2019936117

Publication of this book was made possible by a generous gift from the Meijer Foundation. This work is supported in part by an award from the Michigan Council for Arts and Cultural Affairs.

Wayne State University Press
Leonard N. Simons Building
4809 Woodward Avenue
Detroit, Michigan 48201–1309

Visit us online at wsupress.wayne.edu

Contents

I

Oh, Splotch of Blue Paint

Caribbean Sea blue in the center
of cream-colored sidewalk outside
the Auto Shop classroom.

How you delight me on this Day Six
of the new school year, the sky above
a gentler, more timid shade of your burst.

Oh, blue splotch, are you a foreshadowing
of the year to come? A disruptive blast
set to smash the bulletproof monotony

of the dull grey days? Oh, splotch of aqua-
marine blue, from whose bucket did you
splatter? An art class? Some kid devising

an ocean oasis he wished he could escape
to amidst the morass of too many tests
and terms to define, of auditions for orchestra

seats and not enough sleep and parents hassling
about clothes on the floor, and none of the texts
you thought clever returned? Oh, student splotched

in your own hue of blue, the crying Jordan meme
is you, you, in your despair, have become the crying
meme, and were you trying to paint the sea? A place

for you to float in? The breeze a lovely, reassuring
friend who brings you cookies and iced tea
and listens to you without judging, which is

exactly what the breeze feels like today,
on the sixth day of the school year? Do you
imagine the sun on your cheek the kind

of warmth that hints but does not overpower,
much like the sun the way it is right now?
Did you run out of time due to your dreaming?

Was the bell imminent and you stuck
with a bucket of unused paint that would
dry and cake over the weekend and so had to be

unceremoniously dumped and you chose
the sidewalk instead of the sink? And now
outside of auto class, the sea-blue tendrils

reach across the harsh and boring sidewalk
almost all the way to the unkempt weedy grass,
but they don't quite get there, do they? Oh, splotch

of blue paint, did you hunger
to envelop the whole school, blob
your way through the cafeteria,

the basement wrestling room, the chemistry
labs, the planetarium, the teacher in the pressed
shirt and striped tie lecturing about Salem witches?

Oh, splotch of blue paint, how far did you want
to extend your tropical touch? How much did you
want to add to our already overburdened

backpacks? We need you, splotch of blue paint,
though not today, when the day is already
a bouquet of lush fruit. Will you sustain

your vivid splash, I want to know, after a battalion
of feet have tramped over you during a fire drill?
Will you still be here, trilling your seaside song

come surly March, when the wind and rain
slice their knives and it's been week after week
of waking before dawn, and too many stories

of girls not eating and being forced to their knees
and told to keep quiet about it, too many boys
with fathers never home, or drunk and swinging

when they are, too many defeats and car accidents
and missed assignments and confiscated phones
and nasty hissing whispers and the weight, the weight,

the leaden weight of the year and its unrelenting churn?
Splotch of blue paint, today, Day Six, you smile bright,
you tease and flirt, but where will you be five months

from now when frozen mud stretches to smother you?
Will you be strong enough to melt its knuckled punch
and shine your blue? Will you, paint-splotch, will you?

It's strange

attempting something new at age fifty,
being told, *if you're the driver scheduled*
to leave early, you have dishes, and early
means 2 a.m. instead of 4 and you saunter
head high into the dish room with pots
and buckets and pans sauce-stained
and stacked like towers of tires
and, yes, you can see sponges and steel
wool and three different sinks, but you have
no idea what to do next. What goes where,
which sink fills with what? Soak, then soap,
then rinse, then sanitize sounds logical, but how
to do that, and where does anything go to dry,
how long are you supposed to be at this, don't
you have deliveries to make, shouldn't you be
catching the pies fluming from the oven, affixing
labels to boxes, heading out to knock on someone's
door?

It's not that you mind washing dishes.
You have lived long enough to understand
no work is beneath you, but you at least
like to know how to do what you're doing.

You're used to being in charge of the class,
to meting out doses of knowledge, planning
the lives of your students in fifty-six-minute
intervals. Now, here you are, in collared polo
with company logo, matching baseball hat
and dirtyish white shorts, and you don't
know how to attack a task that should be
fifth-grade easy.

Instead, you'll have to shuffle back to the main portion
of the storefront, be patient as your manager—who used
to be your student—takes a phone order—which is another
thing you don't know how to do—and then you'll have
to ask for advice. You'll have to say what too many
of your tenth graders—whom you always assumed
didn't give a damn—say whenever you open up the laptop
cart and tell them it's time to work on their essays: I *don't
know how to do this. Can you help me? I can't get started.
I'm lost.*

Today for the first time I notice

The Pat Battey Tree. She died what—eight,
ten years ago? A math teacher, and cancer

and I taught her daughter in Creative Writing.
Today, the thrum of industrial air conditioning

overwhelms and I am grateful for its keeping
my too-heavy bulk from drenching itself

with sweat. Outside, I write in the building's
shade, the sky above a leisurely stroll, last class

of the day, and a student teacher prances
past on her way home, headed to the good

lot with abundant parking. All smile
and fashionable haircut, she drags

behind her a wheeled book bag filled
with the day's quizzes and essays.

She is, I'm sure, unaware the tree
I'm sitting next to is the Pat Battey

Tree, or that Pat and I sat next to each other
once at a staff meeting and worked together

in a pair-share according to specification. I'd say
I wish I could remember what we talked about,

but it was probably of little consequence, each
of us exhausted, wishing we could be home

with our own kids after a full day with everyone
else's. She had a complicated laugh, as did her

daughter who, even before her mother fell ill,
wrote poems about how she cut her forearms

with a safety pin. It's a hard thing, high school.
I've been teaching twenty-one years, and still

don't really understand how it works. Pat's illness
progressed quickly. One day she was lecturing

about polynomials; a few weeks later, the math
department was dedicating a tree in her memory.

That sounds horrible to say. I've taught thousands
of classes since her death. In fact, I teach a thousand

classes every forty weeks. A school year is thirty-
nine. Not quite a thousand classes, but almost.

This is what I want to say to the student teacher
with the rolling book bag. *Are you ready to teach*

a thousand classes? Tomorrow, your students
will be at their desks, peering at you, waiting

for you to lead them,

waiting, waiting

for you.

Making the first milkshake

I.

I've been warned. The other Jeff
who's my age, maybe a year or three
older, screwed it up big-time. He only

drives 'til midnight, then departs
to work his next job, bagging copies
of *The New York Times* and delivering

them before dawn. In fact, my house
is part of his route. Twice now, I've
arrived home at 5 a.m., at exactly

the precise moment he—through the pass-
enger-side window of his beat-up van—
tosses our morning paper onto the driveway.

We are, in that moment, a fog-smudged Venn
diagram of two middle-aged Jeffs colliding
as we captain our weathered vessels through

the sea of un-time when bedroom windows
remain darkened, undergrads smoke themselves
to oblivion and traffic lights cease to function.

The other Jeff is friendly and wears the kind
of white hair and mustache I associate
with youth baseball coaches. He also has

a daughter, maybe a year or three older
than mine. He's told me how he and her
mother disagree whether she should be

able to see certain R-rated movies. I did
not mention how my daughter, at age
thirteen, used the c-word in a poem.

Here's the thing. Retrieving *The New York*
Times from its blue hot dog bun of a bag
is the first task I undertake each morning

when I leave the house to commence my work-
day, the one where I instruct a hundred-and-forty-
plus students on the most effective way to create

transitions between body paragraphs, the one
where I'm now a school-wide union rep responsible
for updating the entire staff on contract negotiations,

the one where I quiz students on vocabulary words
like *assiduous, diligent* and *sacrosanct*. I slip the paper
from its casing in order to retrieve the front section.

Often, I immediately open to the editorial
page, just so I can preview how I'll kick-
start my revival at the gym, which columnists

I'll look forward to reading as I pedal
for twenty-seven minutes and twenty-
seven seconds on the stationary bicycle.

When the other Jeff delivers the paper
in the exact slim moment I arrive home
and attempt to untangle my cartilage

from the string theory of the pizza universe,
any hope of effectively transitioning
the paragraphs of my own body vanishes.

I don't know how to take my delivery-guy
face off and gather myself for school
when the same dude who, hours earlier,

helped me carve party trays of extra-cheeses
into twenty-four rectangular-shaped slices,
tosses me my morning paper.

II.

When Pete, the assistant manager, urges me to concoct
my first peanut butter chocolate milkshake, he chuckles
and says the other Jeff, when he lost his milkshake virginity,

proved an apocalyptic fiasco. Ice cream and shake mix flew
around the front counter and all over Jeff's navy polo. Sticky
chocolate syrup made a harrowing tar pit on the floor. I am

determined to avoid such calamities and pay close attention
when Pete shows me, step by step, how to sculpt a milkshake
that will compel our customers to exhort from their dormitories

the glories of our phenomenal service, or, at the very least,
tweet our culinary brilliance to their part-time professors
and tenured thesis advisors. I try to do exactly what Pete

does, but, you know, why not add just a smidgen extra
syrup, a tad more peanut butter, escalate the customer's
experience to a more sublime level of orgiastic ecstasy?

The result—catastrophe.

Peanut butter sprays my face, chocolate syrup stripes
my eyebrows. Ice cream erupts, paints half the store
and all of me. The floor is an arctic tundra, the milkshake

machine a newly formed glacier. I mount a sled and harness
a troupe of snarling huskies and Iditarod-race in quest
of paper towels, rags, my hat, my shirt, anything that can

stem the incipient ice age from layering the continent.
Pete collapses in a stock market crash of laughter.

You Jeffs, he says, *you're all alike.*

My daughter can't find her field hockey jersey

It's game day, the shoes on my feet a gift from my sister.
They're ugly, fit poorly. Good entertainment for my students.
She's nervous, my daughter. Anxious her coach won't let her
play, or if she does, that she won't score goals.

Once I caught a fly ball deep in the right field corner
and ran across the foul line into a drainage ditch.
Held onto the ball but couldn't climb out. A runner
tagged and scored all the way from second base.

A great play, and a horrible one, at the same time.
A student tries to write something, crumples it,
abandons three mostly blank pages in a clump
by a fire hydrant. Doesn't start over. She lost

her lacrosse jacket two springs ago, my daughter.
Often doesn't do her homework. Somebody plonks
a tennis ball with the fat part of the racket. Hits it
perfect. Lord, I love that music.

Who stole the remote?

You want to believe your students respect you enough
not to snicker and watch you squirm through the hour.
You want the crime solved without having to get rough.

Your desk a disaster, crowded with ill-tempered, un-corrallable stuff.
Still, who is bold enough to rifle through this symbolic seat of power?
You want to believe your students respect you enough.

Is it the sneaky boy in the corner, the kid in the hoodie all buff?
The dude on the couch cringing and shy like a delicate flower?
You want the crime solved without having to get rough.

Behind their watery faces are they all laughing as you huff and you puff?
Mocking as you try to teach villanelles from your ivory tower?
You want to believe your students respect you enough.

If you say you'll summon the Principal, will they chortle, call your bluff?
The atmosphere, your rapport, the whole day's growing sour.
You want the crime solved without having to get rough.

Come on, you're a wrestler, you know how to be tough.
What a bummer to have to stand up here, mutter and glower.
You want to believe your students respect you enough.
You want the crime solved without having to get rough.

Dough tray

Dough sticks to the dough tray.
If allowed to dry, it will hold

on fiercely. When wet, it slides
right off. Sometimes a little steel

wool must be invited to the family
gathering to coax the dough from

the plastic surface, but often lukewarm
water suffices to do the sticky job

of unsticking. Then the dough will
dissipate, like the early fire of love,

or any particular stretch of five minutes.
Mostly, it will dive toward the sink drain.

Sometimes it seems like a chunk has
tentacles that try to cling to the rim

of the drain before the body of the beast
spirals downward, but that never works.

Eventually, water always overwhelms.
Eventually, all trays are clean. Stacked.

Trucked back to the regional warehouse
for re-use. Eventually, the store closes.

New dough will arrive the next morning.
Clean hands will roll and stretch it. The oven

will bend its shoulder to its hot work. I will catch
a cascade of pies, box and deliver them. Someone

will say, *this is good pizza. You guys do a good job
over there.* Then will squint, ask, *Did my son have*

you years ago for Tenth Grade English? He did,
didn't he? He remembers that class fondly. Yeah,

you guys do a good job over there. I don't think
I've ever had to wait more than a half hour

for delivery. Not even during a football game,
not even during Hash Bash, not even during

the presidential debates.

Something extra

Think 3:30 a.m., and, Good Lord, who orders pizza that late,
let alone a deep-dish pepperoni and a two-liter of Cherry Pepsi?

Think battered, arthritic knees and dew already spreading its beard
on the grass and you're wandering around a housing development

where the GPS ushers you to the general locus of the development,
but leaves you to your own non-satellite-connected faculties

to navigate deep inside the maze of cul-de-sacs and it's darker
than a coal mine inside a bat cave at the bottom of the iced-over

Arctic ocean and nobody's got lit-up numbers on their front door,
not a single damn house, and the almost invisible numbering system

is additionally as confusing as the boxed set of directions telling
you how to put your life back together, and you've called the phone

number on the receipt—Marley, the name says—and you wonder
if the namesake was the singer who spun a cheery trio of non-

predatory birds of diminutive stature bleating *don't worry* while
sitting on a doorstep they clearly did not have trouble locating, or

Dickens's banker Jacob Marley—wandering phantom and partner
to Ebenezer Scrooge—warning of the folly of wasting earthly

moments like this one at 3:30 in the morning in pursuit
of a handful of extra dollars, and you feel like a ghost now

stuck in a perdition of soaked socks and tennis shoes, trying
to keep the bag holding the slowly cooling pizza parallel to the ground

as you vainly dial Marley's number for the fifth time, then the sixth,
and the void offers no answer and you leave another plaintive message,

your voice echoing and alone, alone—*Hi, again, it's Jeff again,*
from Cottage Inn, again, and I'm just wondering, again, where

I can find you, again. I've got your delivery, again, everything you need,
and I can't find you and I'm fifty and I should be sleeping with a bank

account that's sturdy, but none of that is true, except for the fifty part,
that happened, I became that, just a couple weeks ago, and here I am

trying to find you at the tapering end of this dark, wet night,
can you meet me, can you find me, it's Jeff, again, from Cottage

Inn, again, I've got your delivery, again, can you help me
find you? I'm here. I'm here. And you happen to walk past

a driveway, and a door happens to open, and Marley happens
to see you and she's calling your name through the otherwise

darkness, *Cottage Inn, Cottage Inn, I'm so sorry, my phone was*
off, Cottage Inn, I'm so sorry, I'm here. And you say, no problem,

as you lope—if it's possible for a man with broken knees embarking
upon his sixth decade to lope—up the driveway, it's all good, here's

your pizza, deep-dish pepperoni, right? And she says again she's sorry,
but she's looking at you like you should also be apologizing when all

you did was slog your dead-dog-exhausted third-job-having self for twenty
minutes through wet grass in order to find her—actually her and her

boyfriend, who's standing right next to her in a replica football jersey
looking previously well-fed and basically genial—when a lot of other

drivers would already have said forget it after, at most, three phone calls,
and headed back to the storefront, but you didn't give up, you hate giving

up, you wanted to find her, and now you have, so what in God's name
do you have to apologize for and then it hits you and you're saying,

I'm sorry, I'm sorry, I'll be right back, I left the two-liter in the car,
be right back. Which, of course you won't be, you parked pretty far

away, somewhere not remotely close, in this labyrinthine sequence
of dead-end circles and you sort of remember where the car is

and you do what you can to affect the motion of busted-knees jogging,
in that moment nothing is as important as retrieving the two-liter

from your passenger seat, but you stumble the wrong way, then
the right way, then the wrong again, and somehow you find your car,

drive it back to the house after seven or eight minutes and all you
have become is an apology, a limping, foot-soaked, overly soft flesh-bag

of I'm-sorry-I'm-so-sorry, when you finally hand the two-liter
    to the boyfriend
silhouetted in the doorway while the woman—let's say the two of them

are in their mid-twenties, but let's be honest, you really have no goddamn
idea and just want to head back to the storefront and wash dishes for an hour

so you can try and clock out by five so you can garner maybe 45 minutes
of snooze before you have to take Julius to his 7 a.m. hockey practice—

and Marley-of-the-turned-off-phone has her back to you, her actual rear-
end to you as she bends over against the third or fourth stair on a staircase

and shakes her body—which is encased in only the tiniest of shorts
and the flimsiest emulation of a T-shirt—in what is generally described

as twerking, but in this case is more like a factory in full-blaring fire-force,
one loud piece of machinery clanking into the next, causing a chain reaction

of clanking, chugging, shaking, clanking, tremoring, clanking,
    a particle accelerator
drunk on a volcano-sized vat of caffeine, and you look stone-face straight

at the boyfriend and pretend you don't see the factory in flames,
    the twerking
actually isn't happening, what's important, really, is only the efficient

and highly professional transfer of the two-liter from your hand
to the boyfriend's, your ability to delineate where he needs to sign

the credit card receipt and he says, *what about a tip, where do I put
the tip*, and you point out the designated blank line feeling sheepish,

a tip, you feel, is an idea that should never be acknowledged until after
it's been awarded, and he says to his girlfriend, *how about something extra,*

show him a titty, honey, show him a titty, and you say something to the effect
of, *oh no, really, that's fine, I'm good,* as if you're being offered a second donut

at a department meeting, and he says, *what's wrong, you don't want to see
her titty,* as if he might be mortally insulted if you don't think his girlfriend

is hot enough to lust after and you're fifty with a wife, two kids and a job
where high school students sometimes believe you have wisdom worth

proffering and your sneakers are soaked and goddamnit you just want
to go home, home, please, home, and he's insisting, *come on, honey, show*

him a titty, give him something extra, and, let's be honest, you hate the word
"titty," it makes you squeamish and you can't possibly imagine referring

to your wife's anatomy using the word "titty," nor can you envision proposing
she expose one for the sake of thrilling a moonlighting pizza deliveryman,

and you do your best to shuffle off the porch, signed receipt in hand,
        and head
back to your car, except, you don't quite make it, do you? You are determined,

like Satchel Paige taught you, not to look back, not to ever look back,
but you just can't help it, can you? Like Lot's wife, you turn, you turn,

you cannot avoid turning and looking, who knows why you do it, you're
not excited or curious or anything, really, other than exhausted and maybe

afraid, but you turn nonetheless and there she is, tugging one side
        of her T-shirt
up to her neck, showing you one breast, which really, you don't actually
        see much,

it's a bit like the Janet Jackson wardrobe malfunction,
        did it really happen, was
the greater part of the Judeo-Christian kingdom upset about something
        that flashed

for less than a second, but you chuckle, what the hell,
        it's 3:30 in the morning,
you're in a housing development in dew-soaked sneakers holding an empty

pizza bag and a credit card receipt and something extra just drifted your way,
something extra floated into your cul-de-sac-ed nighttime, your cul-de-sac-ed

career choice, and all you can say is *Beautiful! Awesome! Beautiful!*
        That's, really,
that's, thank you so much for sharing, beautiful, awesome,
        have a wonderful evening.

It seems like you should be more furious the idea for something extra
originated with the boyfriend, not the woman herself, and you damn well

hope the twerking was of her own volition and that maybe when the Jimmy
John's delivery person shows up with subs, she asks the boyfriend

to drop his shorts and offer the sight of something extra from his own
cache of commodities, all you know is, in this moment, you want nothing

more than for this woman to feel like she is everything the earth was born
to bless with all its astonishing splendor, she's beautiful, and awesome,

and generous and much appreciated, the pre-dawn morning has furnished
a supremely awkward miracle. The pre-dawn morning is not the time

for extra-large pepperoni deep-dish, or for a fifty-year-old man
who just wants to go home to be flashed by a woman half his age,

but let us nonetheless celebrate the magnificence of a bare breast
at the tail end of a dark wet night, at the tail end of a relentless,

grinding week, let us celebrate the adventure of a pizza man lost
and then found, of a two-liter forgotten, then retrieved, of wet

sneakers that will soon enough dry; if your wit were more spry
and you were Robert Frost, you'd probably say something

profound and deep like miles to go before you sleep, miles to go
before you sleep, but the truth is the miles are few and you'll

traverse them by car, not horse, but listen, the dishes have piled
up back at the store while you've been wandering around

and getting twerked at and flashed, the dishes, you understand
with a heaviness that won't retreat, the dishes, you understand,

as you lumber back to the street, the dishes, you understand—
you forever understand—are many.

II

Classroom door open

and a student from last year
walks by while we're deeply
immersed in our weekly vocab
quizzing. He's taller now, his shirt
fits the shelf of his shoulders
with less droop. How do ten
weeks of summer change
so much?

The quiz, a half-decade old,
dotters, its Hannah Montana
jokes wheezing. Still, I push it
like an old wheelbarrow stuffed
with fresh soil. Spread enough
around, something can still
bloom. I don't believe in the new
technology, individualized quizzes
with each silent kid stickered
to his own computer screen.
I want community. We learn
a dozen words in chorus, pronounce
them aloud, fill in the blanks as if
we're attending a boisterous town
hall meeting. This is the moment

last year's student struts by, cocks
his head toward the doorway, smiles
sideways as if to say, *I'm past all*
that now, thank God, but thank
God too, that was me last year.
I know what tenth grade will bring
those kids sitting there for the next
nine months, at least I've learned
that much. You keep pushing
that wheelbarrow, Mr. Kass. Keep
spreading those stale dumb jokes.
Keep pushing, keep spreading.

The upside-down remote-control doorstop

works better than almost anything else
in my life. Its rubber buttons adhere
to the hallway's slick linoleum with
the steadfastness of a freshman boy's
crush on his fidget spinner. Which is
to say, that sucker doesn't let go. When
I prop open the door, it *stays* propped.

Do not minimize this paragon of success.
Each day, after I hustle my pathetic
knees up to the third floor, say hello
to the three business teachers—whose
names I invariably mix up if I attempt
to formulate my greeting in any more
specific manner than a generic, *morning
everybody*—and try to beat the bell
to my classroom, the sight of that beat-up,
battery-less remote hanging out in its re-
purposed box of file folders, reassures me
the day will proceed, will march from 2nd
hour through 7th, and I too will stay
propped—upright, or open—or otherwise
able to allow breath to circulate in, around
and straight through whatever I endeavor.

Purveyor of pies

after Jeff McDaniel

Yes, I will interrupt your life.
Knock on your door, or call
your phone, and chances are
we don't know each other, have
no idea which channels our televisions
kiss most frequently, or how many times
the image of our bodies buried in dirt
renders us unable to sleep.

Yet, I know what you want to eat
and at what time you made
your definitive decision to order.
Nobody's day is easy. If, tonight,
you don't want to sift through
the pantry, see what you can
cobble together; if, today,
you did not have time to shop
for groceries; if, this evening,
you just have a hankering
for a medium Barbecued Chicken
with Sweet Baby Ray's, cranberries
and red onions—know I am not
here to judge.

Your life is your own. I will
interrupt it, yes, but only
for brief moments. We will
meet on your doorstep, or
in the apartment foyer;
perhaps your dog will bark
or attempt an escape
to the beckoning wild;

perhaps your toddler
will answer the knock and look
at me with eyes both excited
and afraid. I, a stranger
at the gate, mean only
the opposite of harm, mean

only I am here, arrived, more
or less on time, to provide
you with sustenance, to let
you know when you desired,
we did our best to fulfill. When
I leave, you will shut your door,
return your world to its ordered
momentum, the only alien
infiltration easily digestible,
its cardboard container easily
recyclable. I will move on
to the next house, the next
dorm, the next apartment
complex and interrupt
another life. I am here.

You conjured
and I appeared.

I don't take yearbook photos anymore

Ignore orders at the advent of each September
to report to the cafeteria where a mercenary
photographer sets up camp to capture staff.

In my first year of teaching, a veteran
teacher stood by the photocopier and wept
the day the new yearbooks were released.

We grow older every year, she said, grading
her picture, *and everyone watches it happen.*
I looked up from lesson planning and wanted

to weep too, but never thought I'd teach
more than five years. It's been 23 and I'm
still refusing the elevator, limping up

the stairwell each morning. When I stare
at the washroom mirror in the storefront
at midnight, I see a man most customers

would never suspect has teenage children.
He doesn't look tired, kind of goofy, sure,
and his shirt's too tight, his hair fluffing

like cotton candy beneath his hat.
Still, most customers aren't likely
to suspect much about any driver.

Nor do we suspect much about them.
If they don't tip well, or complain,
we believe they're inhuman. That's it.

You know who tips well? Anyone
working a job who seems to recognize
we also are working a job—police officers,

apartment doorpeople, restaurant
workers, construction workers, nurses,
electricians and phone-repair folks—I don't

avoid eye contact with people
like that, don't mind my jowls
growing meatier, my vision foggier,

my ears and nose expanding like tumors.
But face it, an annual mugshot does no one
any service. Who says the world needs

visual documentation of my decline?

Marty blows up

In Government class, he and his peers watch a video—
Donald Trump on *The View*, arguing why he doesn't trust
Obama's birth certificate. Whoopi Goldberg fires back
loud and angry, but the white women on the show stay
silent, mouths and hands folded, above the fray. *That nipped
at me,* Marty says. *If he's being racist, how come only Black
people seem to care?*

Marty's got glasses and talks with his hands and sometimes
eats lunch in my classroom and likes to describe complex anime
narratives, or Super Smash Bros strategies, while I sort of pay
attention. *It's kind of like,* Marty goes on, *when a teacher picks
on a Black kid who's got his phone out, and the white kids texting
under their desks don't say anything. They just keep on doing
what they're doing. It's like whatever the teacher's saying*

to the Black kid

*has nothing to do
with them*

at all.

Wrong city ghazal

You're called to deliver an order to Linwood Street.
Traffic tangles, rain mangles, you search for the thin good street.

A woman cursed your manager after another driver failed.
Now he assigns you the task—locate her dim, rude street.

You circumnavigate, the GPS prevaricates, you scan dark
un-numbered homes. There's no 905 Linwood Street.

The customer curses your call—*What the fuck's wrong
with you? I'm out here waiting on Linwood Street.*

You exit your car. Look left. Right. No one. Nothing. Cold
air like pliers on your neck on this no-win lewd street.

You ignore the *why the hell are you doing this* in your brain,
use your most polite voice, *are you sure you're on Linwood Street?*

*Yes, I'm sure, you frickin' douche. What are you, stuck
in an alternate universe with a twin 'hood, street?*

A magical emerald appears in your mind—*you are
in Ann Arbor, right? Zip code 48104, on Linwood Street?*

No, asshole, she says, *Kalamazoo,* then she pauses, hangs up.
No apology for ordering food 90 miles from her slim good street

And you, Jeff, stand in the slush, tipless—a half hour
wasted—holding a still full pizza bag on Linwood Street.

Karma's a fuckin' bitch

Joanna says. She's a cook, someone
who rolls dough and makes pizzas,
shows me how to mix ranch dipping
sauce and garlic cream cheese. When
I'm in the backroom and she drops off
a sauce-drenched bucket for me to clean,
she smirks, says, *just when you thought
you were finished,* and it feels like sort
of an apology. When she laughs, the sound
splits the store the way the pizza cutter rolls
through pies and makes slices. She curses a lot.
Not under her breath, or even over it,
but deep within it, owning its symphonic
surge. Calls students who come in drunk
and loud at 3 a.m. and flirt sloppily, who can't
decide what to order, *fucking ass-wipes.*

Calls the regional managers who check
on whether we're sufficiently up-selling
cinnamon sticks and 16-piece chicken wings,
pompous ass-kissing motherfuckers. I don't
think she's older than I am, but her kids are
older than mine. Her ex-husband, she says,
a fuckin' crackhead, stole all her money. She
has no sympathy for the driver who was also
robbed. He bragged about a ninety-dollar tip
the night before, told everyone *as if his lucky
ass somehow deserved it, then somebody broke
into his house, stole nine hundred. See, don't
fuck with Karma, man, just don't fuckin' do it.*

Leonard says his poems got rejected from the youth literary magazine

By way of offering comfort, I say,
Man, I get rejection letters every day,
sometimes three or four of them.

Yeah, he says, *but this is the first*
thing I ever sent my poems to.

Like a knuckle to the nose, it hits
me what he means: my continued
failures do not blunt the spike
of his disappointment.

It's self-indulgent, of course, for me
to think they might, like an old man
who's trudged through a trio of divorces
and tries to tell some kid—who finally summoned
the spine to ask the red-haired siren with green-
sleeved baseball shirt, whom he's been crushing
on for the better part of six consecutive semesters,
to a movie and she said sorry—that, *you know, they're*
not always going to like you, sometimes you just have
to move on, find someone else to like.

The truth is I just don't have
an emotional wellspring deep
enough to mete out the required
cistern of soothing to each
of my hundred-forty-plus
students. Sometimes, I simply
don't give a damn. Some mornings
my car smells too much like hockey
gear and garlic. Some nights I want
to eat a sandwich and watch basketball

on television and forget a stack of essays
in my backpack has lain unloved, untouched
well past its expiration. Some nights
I want to fling all the pizzas like Frisbees
into the middle of a municipal park, let five
hundred pile up like a funeral pyre and blow
them to bits with some kind of sophisticated
firework missile I can't possibly afford
from a roadside pop-up stand in Ohio.

What I'm saying, Leonard,
is I'm sorry for being a grouchy
garbage bag of a person. I wish
your poems had been accepted.
I wish you felt better about
yourself, about the future ducking
and flirting behind the trees in front
of you. Sometimes I wake up and ask
myself, *what am I doing better now
than I've ever done in my life?*

Sometimes the answer is little, or nothing.

I'm sorry that's not comfort either.

Unworthy

My wife says I don't value myself.
She insists there has to be something
else I could be doing. Tutoring, perhaps,
or advising students on college essays.
I could be making fifty, seventy-five
dollars an hour.

It's Christmas Eve. Almost midnight.
Another driver told me he just got stiffed.
Delivered to a house and no one was present.
That's messed up, I say, chuckling at my own
joke, *Christmas Eve, no presence.* He ignores
me, says he called the customer, who asked
if he could meet her at a gas station two miles
away. Drove there, delivered the food—no tip.

I am folding boxes in the parking lot. Stuffing
them into recycling bins. Inside, the general
manager—my former student who did little
work in my class—weighs dough on a scale.
He trooped in after his normal hours to check
inventory. On Christmas Eve. It is balmier than
it should be for late December in Michigan. Maybe
forty degrees. Fog rises like steam off mostly melted
snow. I lean against my battered car, watch
the no-traffic on the street. The humid air.
A slow night, maybe thirty bucks in tips. Not
a lot of dishes in the backroom. Earlier, carolers
knocked on a door and sang to a house across
the cul-de-sac from where I knocked on a door
to deliver a calzone and a two-liter. Streetlights
glow with a hazy aura. It's sort of magical.
The night manager appreciates the fact
I've got my khaki game on lock. I think
I look like I work here.

I'd be lying

If I didn't admit there are some perks.

In the grand concourse of human events,
what feels better than concocting
for one's self a crispy thin-crust opus
that would never appear on the menu?

How about no sauce, but slather a swath
of garlic butter for your savory base?

Spread a fistful of cheddar, some
grated parm, maybe throw in a few
crumbles of feta. Add fresh tomatoes,
enough green olives to feed a middle
school, pickles, a few slender and tender
slices of salami. Mushrooms. Onions.
A battalion of banana peppers. You're
singing now, Bro. Go ahead and slide it

in the oven—that pulmonary engine
of gastro-economy thrumming in the storefront
middle that feeds everything else we do,
that behemoth's working for *you* now,
not for the pleasure of some customer waiting
with a hefty wallet, but for the pleasure of you
and the twelve minutes you'll have to chow down
before howling out on your next run. Head

into the backroom and knock off some dishes
while you're waiting. Attack some dough trays.
Make that backroom glisten. Feel the ache
in your fingers and the chill in your sink-soaked
shirt. The harder you go at it, the better your brilliant
brainchild will taste when it announces its arrival
at the end of its 600-degrees-of-amalgamation
growth spurt. Listen, don't let someone else

pull that pizza out for you. You give yourself
the glory of watching that pièce de résistance,
that chef-d'oeuvre, emerge with all its bubbling
heat from the oven's long and swarthy kiss. Use
the giant spatula and slide it into a box
just like you would a pie belonging
to any paying customer. Give it that
respect. But here's a secret. It's for you
and that means you can slice it

any dang way you want—rectangles, squares,
parallelograms, trapezoids, squircles, heptagrams—
Man, book yourself a cosmic journey to Shapetown,
Shape Mountain, The Shape-terrerean Sea. This pie
is for you. No one else needs to see it or know about it.

Let it cool, let it mature.

Believe

for a moment

your time

belongs

to you.
        Savor.
        Chew.

The manager talks about getting engaged

I think I'm ready, he says. *What was it like for you? Did you
do anything special?* The story is, yes, it was, in fact, special,
but not because of any particular planning, or creative
proposal-ing. It was spontaneous and, actually, I don't
want to talk about it. Despite all my admonitions
to students about vanquishing vagueness, it's not
a story I like to share. It involves Santa Cruz and sea lions
and a tall bearded man playing bagpipes in the midst
of a mournful fog, and that's all I'm going to say.
The story is for me and for Karen and, maybe, one day
for our children. I hold it tight to my chest and I want
to keep it like that, an heirloom.

Except, it's nearing 5 a.m. when he asks,
and I'm mopping the floor. Sort of. It's been
a long, unnerving night, ice and snow and roads
that want to bite, and he's counting money
in the register and accomplishing other mysterious
paperwork-related functions—I think I made
about $105 in tips, add on the 54 cents per mile
and the $5.25 an hour salary and I'm around 180
bucks for eleven hours, not horrible—but the floor
sneers daunting and salty and the water in the mop-
bucket already swims swampy, so I'm swishing back
and forth as quickly as I can but the truth is the world's
not a whole lot cleaner and my arms and upper back feel
like I just survived six minutes of wrestling against a State
Champ, so I'm half-tempted to tell the story just to cheer
my own damn self up.

A university professor earlier tipped five dollars
on a ninety-seven-dollar bill, and he also declined
to meet me at the door in the midst of the snowiest
bluster. Sent down a student clearly unprepared
to schlep seven pizzas (including one gluten-free)

upstairs to the classroom, so I did it for him, an extra
ten minutes of my time while another customer's
delivery camped in the car, and I don't know what
kind of class it was, possibly marketing, something
in the how-to-make-money-by-lying-to-people genre.
About thirty undergrads inhabited the classroom, each
likely capable of chipping in a buck, though none offered,
and I considered making a public announcement exposing
their instructor as a 6% tipper after he asked me a bunch
of bullshit questions like do I get sick of pizza and does
my car smell like pizza and so much of me wanted to say,
listen up, students, the dude here who's grading your papers,
or, more likely, foisting that job onto a graduate assistant who
gets paid little more than expired lettuce, is trying to make nice
with me, act like he recognizes the complexity of my humanity,
but he just tipped 5 bucks on a 97-dollar bill and you do the math,
that adds up to an asshole at the extreme tail of the bell curve
and I got two kids I'm not putting to bed right now, not helping
with their homework, not standing next to in the washroom
as they floss and brush their teeth and I still got nine hours
to go on this shift, then it's sleep two hours and snap my sorry ass
awake for my son's hockey game, so if you learn one lesson this semester—
how about it's every person who's ever served you anything, fed
you or cooked for you, or refilled your coffee or refolded a sweater
you left in a heap after fingering through the bargain rack—every
damn one of them might have a magical story comprised of sea lions
and bagpipes and mournful fog they hold close to their chests?

But I don't say any of that and I feel smaller for it. I want to be
that fiery teacher I once was, unafraid of losing his job, unwilling
to compromise a principled belief or stand in muted silence
when an explosion's brewing in his throat, and the manager's
looking up from his register, his own shoulders looking like
pumpkins three weeks after Halloween, deflated and nibbled
apart by squirrels, and I push the mop harder, try now to make
the floor Cinderella-sparkle, for we who close the store at 5 a.m.
must be our own fairy godmothers, our own Prince Charmings,

there is no one else in this moment for us, no one thinking of us
but us, and I polish that floor so it shines like a glass slipper
and the bark of sea lions lurches upward from hundreds
of feet below the craggy cliffs and it roars onto my tongue;
actually, I say, *special doesn't begin to describe. It was in Santa Cruz
and we were on this bluff and the wind had that kind of chill like somebody
pressing fingernails into the hollow of your back so I gave her my sweatshirt.
It was royal blue with, for some reason, the number 88 sewn onto the front
on a white patch, and we could hear some guy playing bagpipes, sending
his screeching prayer into the mist and down below on the beach sea lions . . .*

*down below on the beach . . . and she looked at me . . . and we
could hear . . . and she started nodding her head and I said
what are you saying yes to? What are you saying yes to?*

But I already knew.

III

The crime

I.

2:30 a.m. on Saturday night and I pull up to South Quad.
Before I even dial my phone to let the customer know
I'll be downstairs, medium sausage-and-mushroom in hand,

a stout beefy man summoned by a college kid who would
never believe students plead I weave recommendation dreams
so they can claim their own frolicking place in this precise

rollicking space, I am ambushed by a blonde woman
who hammers my passenger-side door. Stuffed with
smile and the kind of bounce that vacated my body

decades earlier, she says, *Cottage Inn? Is that
for me?* I'm startled, and she's sloppy drunk,
kin then to ten thousand other students

in the general vicinity so I'm not skeptical.
Are you Carissa? I say. She hesitates, but who
knows what she hears or doesn't or how she's

processing the steamy night around her, the streams
of other inebriates in shorts and tank tops. Is she pretty?
Who the hell knows? She's young and drunk and blonde

and finally says, *Yeah, I'm Carissa,* and I do not doubt.
I believe, like I always want to believe, that people are
who they say they are.

II.

Her friend approaches, another zonkered blonde
with some kind of sleeveless suede vest, the sort
of thing my wife wore when we were twenty-five

and falling in love, students on our own buzzing
campus in New York who believed we'd one day work
satisfying jobs, but never imagined three at once,

and the first one who assaulted
my door says, *it's our pizza.*
He brought our pizza.

The pizza we ordered? Yeah, he brought it. In retrospect, I am
a clueless and delusional dumb-ass, but at the time, I just think,
dang, she's drunker than I thought, hope she can still sign

this credit card receipt and doesn't forget to add a couple
extra dollars—which, you know, two bucks, that's roughly
a third of a sandwich at Jimmy John's—and also, why did

she startle me? Who gave her the right to startle the pizza guy?
Outside, I slide the pie from its heated home; she leans against
the window to sign the receipt and tells her friend, *I'm Carissa.*

Her friend laughs
and dumb-ass me,
I think drunk-ass them.

I do not think thieves.

III.

Off the criminals scuttle, the tip is two bucks,
and, yes, I am as naïve as an eight-year-old
ordering sea monkeys from the back of a comic book.

Two drunk women steal Carissa's pizza and I do not
even suspect foul play until halfway back to the store,
and when the real true authentic Carissa calls twenty

minutes later, hungry, confused, wondering why I have
not shown up to feed her, we—by some gentle karmic
massage—have an extra mushroom-and-sausage straight

from the oven—another customer cancelled moments earlier—
so, instead of hitting the dumpster, it hits my passenger seat
and I bolt back to South Quad—where reliably each weekend

an ambulance will arrive to transport an alcohol-poisoned
reveler to the ER—and this time I make absolutely certain
it's Carissa who meets me. I mean, I even ask her to bring

student ID so I can double-check, and the real true authentic
Carissa is not drunk; in fact, she shows up gracious and un-angry
and pleased as pie about the pie's inevitable, if tardy, arrival

and she's wearing giraffe pajamas, the adult version
of a toddler's onesie, and though it's not the design
of the statuesque 19-foot-tall Maasai, but rather

the slightly less robust Reticulated, still,
she is a patient, kind woman dressed
in tribute to one of the universe's

most majestic creations—who, if you ever saw one
in the wild, looks almost exactly like a walking tree,
a strutting, gamboling, magnificent tree—and did I

mention the two drunk women who felt entitled
to steal another woman's pizza—to impersonate
her and sign her credit card receipt—were both

blonde and both white, and the women waiting
graciously was neither—and, sure, I'd like to say
this is just a funny story, a quirky thing that happened

one night while I was delivering pizzas—a funny thing,
ha ha, let's all inhabit the community of laughing and not
talk about whether our civilization is crumbling, if this

Trumpeting is a last desperate bleat of a dying alabaster
beast, but, look, we've lost 40% of our global giraffe
population over the last three decades, the species

has now been downgraded to *vulnerable to extinction,*
and I once kissed a giraffe. It happened at a giraffe
sanctuary and I stood on a platform with a pellet

of processed giraffe food in my mouth, clutched
between my teeth, and a lovely 16-footer skipped
blithely along and lashed out with its foot-long

tongue and lathered the entire territory of my face
with its saliva and the kiss was warm and wet
and the magnificent creature took its meal right

out of my mouth,

but, listen,

by virtue of my standing on that platform
with the giraffe food protruding as far
outward as I could stretch my own

wrestling-thick neck, I gave the giraffe
implicit permission to eat what was lodged
between my bicuspids. In fact, you could say

the act constituted a preview of my later immersion
in professional food delivery, and you can also insist
the shameless pair of pizza thieves is no metaphor

for the collapse of our collective nationhood. To which
I say, if late-night pizza, *highly anticipated* late-night pizza
—with hand-embellished garlic butter-parmesan crust—

can be pilfered, then what, exactly, do we consider sacred?
If we cannot trust those who reach out with their hands
toward the underpaid, overstressed delivery class are,

in fact, the people
who actually ordered
the food,

who can we trust?

IV.

I have lived more than half my life.
It is easy to dismiss me as obsolete,
too slow on my intellectual feet
to recognize when I'm being scammed.

Or maybe I'm just dunked-lead sunk
in underpaid, overworked self-pity
and take every damn thing too seriously.
But here is a truth. When I navigate the city

to bring you your pizza, that is the end
of a chain of events that begins with your
dialing the number to our store. At any
given moment, your call might interrupt

someone attempting to dent a mound of dishes,
or sprinkle goat cheese evenly across a family-sized
cranberry-walnut salad. You might interrupt someone
cutting a half-pepperoni, half-Hawaiian (kind of a horrible

combination, but it happens), or spreading parmesan
across the skin of a large calzone. All these tasks
are accomplished with care. We never want
a customer to experience the slightest yip

of disappointment. Yet, when the phone rings,
we figure out a way to pause what we're doing
and answer. Regardless of how tired we are,
or what insane hour it is, or how many calls

we've already fielded, we endeavor to be our best,
most radiant human selves—*Thank you for calling
Cottage Inn, how can I help you?* We repeat your order
back to you to make sure we have it right, we repeat

your phone number back to you to make sure we have it right,
we repeat your address back to you to make sure we have it right.
We follow whatever special instructions you provide in regard
to whether you want your pizza well-done (yes, there is such a thing

as a well-done pizza), whether you want light on the sauce,
or gluten-free, or with extra banana peppers. When we make your food,
we offer it the same attention and affection we'd offer a first date, even
if it's the 500th pizza of the day. We do not want to fuck *anything* up.

When we retrieve your pizza from the oven, we box it with a devotion
akin to wrapping a Christmas present for a best friend forever. With
practiced hands, we cut the pie, even and deep, so you can pull each
slice away with ease. We know you are waiting for us, that once you

dialed the phone and made your desire a tangible thing
in the world, a wish to be fulfilled, it is our great privilege—
and I do mean privilege, check out my dude Dylan
with the comforting grin and ballpoint pen stuck

behind his ear, or my dude Kevin with the minivan
and dreadlocks and mid-shift calls to his kids
to tuck them into bed; we can't just do this
for the money, there isn't enough of it—we ache

to make at least one choice you made today work
out the exact way you want it to. We double-check
the ticket to make sure we include all elements
of the order; do we need a milkshake, a two-liter,

a salad, extra Dippin' Cups? We do not want to fuck
anything up. Once we're absolutely sure the order's
ready to go, we pack it in the heat bag, type the address
into the GPS and attempt to find you. *You.* Not someone

who pretends to be you. When we pull out from the parking
lot, often into the midst of angry traffic, we have one purpose.
Connect with *you.* If you're not you, the fragile ecosystem
is at fatal risk. You who claim a pizza that is not your own,

are not just a fraud,
you are a galaxy-ravager,
a Ragnarok, a Death Star.

V.

I need you to be you.

I am fifty years old and exhausted.

I look for meaning in every ice patch on every sidewalk.

I try to hold onto every spark and somehow keep it flickering.

When I head out into the night in my battered vehicle,

food steaming in a navy blue bag on my passenger seat,

I need to believe you summoned me and I will arrive.

You need me and I will provide.

Laugh if you can't feel, but I'm telling you,

the jolt in my blood is no joke.

I need to believe where I'm headed

is where I'm supposed to go.

IV

Young man, take your headphones out

is the refrain of Ian's poem, and the refrain
he hears each morning when he pushes
into the building at 7:30, sleet stinging
his face.

Young man, take your headphones out,
Ian hears, and obeys long enough to move
past the line of sight of the assistant principal
yelling at him through a megaphone, before
he puts them back in.

Young man, take your headphones out,
Ian hears in his sleep, when he eats a foil-pack
of Pop-Tarts for breakfast, as he clambers
onto his bicycle, and, whatever the weather,
rides it to school.

Young man, take your headphones out,
I hear as I pull into traffic, seeing Ian's
anguished face as he sits atop the classroom
radiator, hearing his throaty voice when he
reads his poem, as I half-listen to the radio,
late already, on my way to deliver
my twentieth pizza of the night.

Young man, take your headphones out,
I hear as the first few notes from Whitney
Houston's "I Will Always Love You" play
through the car's speakers and despite
my tardiness, I pull over into a 7–Eleven
parking lot.

Young man, take your headphones out,
Ian repeats as the anchor of his poem,
a custody-sharing tale of three days
a week with his father, and four
with his mother.

Young man, take your headphones out,
as he rides his bike back and forth
between parents, and the only thing he takes
with him everywhere is his music. The only
stability in his life, on his bike, in the hallways,
in his head—his music.

Young man, take your headphones out
disappears as I sit in the parking lot,
engine running, for three minutes,
so I can hear Whitney drag out that
long *ayyyyyyyyyyyyyyyayyyyyayyyyyy,*
about 5/6ths of the way through
the song and how just that single stretched-
out vowel, that one sparkling sound,
will buoy me through the rest of this shift,
maybe the rest of the week, the school year,
who knows, maybe even my whole damn
career.

Territories

I.

Evan says Robert's bullying him, threatening to slug him with his backpack
full of textbooks and, let's be honest, Robert's a big kid. His shoulders could
be mini fridges, his fists padlocks. Evan's jumpy. The kind of kid who won't
slaughter a spider, or even a mosquito, but will capture either in a paper cup
and cart it outside.

In the hallway, where I've summoned him during class so he can't perform
before an audience of peers while I scold him, Robert tells me, *he stole
my seat. You know I have anger issues. That's why I separate myself,
so I can stay calm. I go back there in the corner and make my own space.
He can't just sneak in and steal that from me.*

True, but, you still can't threaten to smack him with your backpack.

Well, I wouldn't do it if he just let me sit where I always sit.

Other teachers gaze at me now, poke their heads from their rooms
at the hint of heat in the corridor. Can the Assistant Principal down
    the hall
hear us from his office? I lower my voice, try to sound like the kind
    of background
music that plays in a high-end supermarket. All right, I say, how
about, just for today, you sit somewhere else? I'll talk to Evan
after class about how important that seat is to you, but you
need to promise if you're feeling angry, for whatever reason,
you'll come talk to me instead of threatening anyone, deal?

Robert says nothing. Yanks the hood of his sweatshirt up, his eyes floorward.
A kid in the Robotics Club wearing an 8.5 x 11-inch
laminated hall pass around his neck that says, *I surrendered
to defeat because I don't care enough about missing valuable
instructional minutes so I chose not to be patient enough
to use the bathroom after the bell* walks by, his eyes radar-
locked on the battlefield pixelated on his phone.

Deal?

Nothing.

A guidance counselor in a purple T-shirt that proclaims in white text across
her back, *Lead, Care, Aspire*, scurries past and tosses me a question with
her eyebrows.

Deal?

Nothing.

Deal?

Nothing.

I can't allow you back into the classroom if you can't promise me.

His eyes don't move from the floor, but the sweatshirt hood nods.

Or, maybe, I just
want to believe

it does.

II.

Tonight, electricity abandons the Cottage Inn store in the north part of
town.
Their calls get re-routed to us and then the swarm shows up, a vibrating
six-pack of drivers, one after another skidding into our lot. The last drives
a Prius, the light blue shade I didn't want to wait the extra ten days for
when I settled on mahogany, and it boasts no dents or duct tape. Their manager
and our manager huddle, then issue a joint edict: *Plymouth Road drivers take
deliveries in their area, Packard drivers take deliveries in theirs.*

Fair enough, but the parking lot's too crowded, looks like Football Saturday
at the corner of Main and Stadium. No room to back out while punching
an address into the GPS and balancing

a milkshake
on top of a salad on top
of a feta cheesebread,
on top of a large Pepperoni.

Let them take their Plymouth runs,
but do they have to clog our lot's
plumbing

to do it?

Inside, the store's a mosh pit of obstetricians. Nowhere to move without
   jostling somebody's elbow or the isthmus of a hip bone. Eight of us
   wait for our thrumming double-time oven to push out its progeny.
   We all display our retrieving, slicing, crust-flavoring and boxing-up
   skills, try to earn the Gold Medal of Quick Draw McGraw Pizza
   Master Maestro. We don't ask about children, other jobs, why people
   vote against their own economic self-interest. It's all *take Fifth, not
   Fourth. Cut across Thompson. Avoid the construction on Division.* We share
   information but only in a way that says, *we know what we know
   because we're better than you.*

III.

Dear Mr. Kass & Principal Korver—over the weekend,
Evan related to us how tense his 4th hour has been.
He said he left class to go into the hall angry one day
because he could not take it anymore. He was speaking
about TH and F of last week, days on which Mr. Kass met outside
with at least other one student due to classroom behavior.
Evan said that on one of the days, he was trying to be "courageous"
and try

a new seat

(something he'd already tried with backlash from peers)

a student came in,

saw "his seat" taken by Evan.

The student then swung his backpack

in Evan's direction and let it go.

It crashed under a desk

right near Evan and bothered him

quite a bit.

If you could both please check out this situation and help Evan negotiate
trying "new" things but also ones that will lead to positive results,
it would help him. Evan is frustrated with the times the focus is not
on learning. Perhaps, quite a challenging group.

There is still a month-plus to go in the semester.

Evan mentioned there is another adult

in the room

but was not able to give

much information

about how or if

s/he is able

to assist students

or Mr. Kass.

Emma broke her friend's arm
by hitting her with a pillow

She tells us the story when I welcome everyone
back for the new year, ask if anything interesting
happened over break. Actually, it was just a dislocation,
not a break, a shoulder popping out of its socket, but she
went straight from goofy sleepover mode to parent mode,
from socking her buddy with a soft, foamy implement of slumber
to comforting her, calling for an ambulance.

She likes that about herself.

It's strange what we like about ourselves. How I see the white
in my hair and appreciate its shyness, how it creeps slowly
into prominence. Maybe more of me could be like that. A quiet
presence that ultimately fills the room, everyone else sitting around,
eating supermarket cookies, then here I am—*has he always been
there?*—and everyone's listening and the staff meeting ends up being
more interesting than the staff had any right to expect.

Nothing about the next ten minutes is promised.

A pillow can separate a shoulder.

A baby can hop from its crib
and make its way downstairs
and a mother watching television can say,

*how did you
get here?*

What if my ankle twisted into a knot right now?

Would I like myself
      from the ground
      up?

Sestina for the segregated class

It seems impossible, a ferocious task—
to compel the white girls crackling in the corner
to connect to the stoners huddled on the couch to the left,
or to get the gender-fluid quartet laughing in the back
to heed the African American sextet flanking the window,
or melt the ice with the hockey players skating through the middle.

I want the world to work without a seating chart in its middle,
but the class grows no closer as we muddle from task to task.
I look toward the sky, hope a strategy floats through the window,
but I feel like a battered boxer, bleeding in his corner,
wondering how he can muster the strength for a comeback
when the world pummels and jab-hooks right vs. left.

My brain's an empty refrigerator, no nourishing ideas left.
Perhaps, I could kneel on the floor in the classroom middle,
plead from my knees for each student to banish to the back
of their worries any heebie-jeebies resulting from the task
of emerging from the cocoon of their corners
and letting someone else breathe through the windows

of their lives. I've grown older and more fearful, still the window
of mine seems less fragile. If someone new floats through, what's left
standing gives proof, a stone column bolstering each corner
of this half-century-old bastion. No longer seventeen with sturdy middle,
I nonetheless claw forward and finish the task.
If I can communicate any truth worth giving back,

let it be that the grip of the invisible goblin holding you back
is no less breakable than a cut-glass window.
You can shatter it with the careening baseball of your free will. Task
yourself to wrestle any distress you have left,
be that intrepid linebacker who caretakes the middle,
tackles every dread, roams confident from corner to corner.

I'm sorry for these mismatched metaphors plucked from the corner,
these fun-housed bromides reflected sideways and back,
but this class is a huddle of vegetables circling the dip in the middle
and we need to dive in and smear the windows
with the communal food fight of our fears until all that's left
is a messy, chunky goulash; florid, spicy and up to the task

of rounding sharp corners and splashing light through each window.
We can have each other's backs, pull from the right, left
and middle, braid a vibrant quilt of our stories. That is our task.

A colleague says sometimes he thinks anyone who's been married more than five years deserves a medal

Monday morning and we hover by the photocopier
in the third-floor Language Arts office, anxious between
2nd and 3rd hour classes, duplicating handouts we should
have prepared the previous Friday.

Through the window, a cross street intersects Stadium Blvd.
in a perfect T, both sides of the thoroughfare jammed with
recycling bins. The street seems like an escape route. I watch
for several seconds; no cars traverse it. *How long have you
been married?* I ask, a question that suggests an easy answer,
compared to, say, *are you okay?*

He says three years. I'm quiet again. Watch the non-traffic
on the T. A truck will lumber along at some point, grab
the bins with forklift hands, plunder them, then return them
to their curbside upright positions. We all have our problems.
I chin-nod toward the copier where his handouts cascade out-
ward, collated and stapled. *What are you teaching?*

Kindred, he says, and *Death of a Salesman.* I'm familiar with
the second story, the unhappy man with a going-nowhere son
named Happy and a lover he embraces in motels. *I've never
read Kindred*, I say. *Students like it? Love it*, he says. *What's not
to love about traveling back in time to find out who you are?*

I travel backward to Friday afternoon when I failed to prepare
the lesson I'm teaching today. It's a new one, not recycled.
We'll read a long poem about parents cheering when their
children suck at basketball, how mothers and fathers unite
the bleachers to conjure a robust cloud of love

in the gymnasium air, a thick scent of love, while their sons
turn the ball over and get stomped. I'll ask students to write
about an experience where they've felt love like that, palpable
and thick, with a smell, kidnapping the air. Three weeks

remain until Spring Break. I merit no bleacher cheers
for how I've behaved in my marriage, but it's still upright,
seventeen years deep, no matter how many times it's been
hollowed out, refilled.

Against automatic hand dryers

after Rita Dove

Of course, I believe in best sanitary practices.
Students and teachers must wash hands thoroughly
after using the restroom and nobody wants moistened palms
dripping through hallways or staining vocabulary quizzes.

Too, I'm all for saving trees. If we can dispense with thousands
of reams of paper towels—many of which also wind up
dripping their way down the hallway—yes, absolutely,
I vote affirmative. And yet, with my classroom

permanently anchored next to the Boys' washroom
the constant burst of *whooshrzzzzzahrrrggggzzzz-
zahhhhhhhshhhhhh* sounds like the opening and re-opening
and opening and re-opening and closing and re-opening

and opening and closing and re-opening of pneumatic
doors to a subway car and cuts like a hacksaw deli-slicing
skin off the side of my skull. Why don't I just shut my door?
Yes, but the room hosts a south-facing bank of windows

and a heating-and-cooling system as unreliable as my rear-
wheel-driving hybrid in a snowstorm, which means if I don't
keep my door open, we deep-fry like a twelve-pack of Twinkies
at a state fair, and, listen, we're reading about Piggy now,

the dramatic moment when Roger smashes him with a boulder
and he becomes not an asthmatic boy with fire-starting glasses
but the true wise friend falling sideways to his death, or we're
reading about Holden, how he grows unbearably sad gazing

at the green of a young prostitute's dress hanging in the hotel
closet. Listen, there's a poem *whooshrzzzzzahrrrggggzzzz-
zahhhhhhhshhhhhh* right now and the student who wrote it
whooshrzzzzzahrrrggggzzzzzahhhhhhhshhhhhh needs us

to pay *whooshrzzzzzahrrrggggzzzzzahhhhhhhshhhhhh* attention. It's a matter of life and no else ever has, and all she needs is for us to *whooshrzzzzzahrrrggggzzzzzahhh-hhhhshhhhhh* tune in and let her know *whooshrzzzzz-*

ahrrrggggzzzzzahhhhhhhshhhhh someone cares enough *whooshrzzzzzahrrrggggzzzzzahhhhhhhshhhhhh* to listen.

James waves at me
in the middle of the night

He sells real estate by day
drives Uber after dark
says he's only had one
drunk student throw up
and the kid opened the door
first, managed to hit the street
with most of it.

Our sons played hockey
together and we stood
behind the glass watching
them skate. He taught me
what icing the puck means
and how to appreciate a good
coach when your kids have
one. *Sometimes,* he tells me,
I drive until three, pull over
in a parking lot when people
are done coming home from
the bars, nap a couple hours,
wake up and, especially Monday
mornings, start driving people
to the airport before work.

Uber won't accept me as a driver,
too many speeding tickets, most
accrued on the way to hockey practice.
It's crazier for you, he says, *doing dishes*
in the backroom 'til 5, then going to school.
Me, I love the kids. When they're drunk,
after all, someone has to get them
home safe. My daughter texts me
on nights I'm on shift, right before

she goes to sleep. *Drive safely,* she
writes. *You're the best dad ever.* I'm
not, but I do think about making sure
I'm at the table, eating breakfast
when she wakes up. *Get home safely,*
I tell myself, when I'm backing
out into traffic. I think of James
waving when we pass each other
at an intersection, traffic lights
sleepy with their yellow blinks.
Whatever else, get home safe.

Outside the window

the softball team warms up. Players toss the ball back
and forth, field grounders, shag flies. Their speaker
system plays Rihanna—*there's something about*
that work, work, work, work, work. School

ends in six minutes, then it's hustle to the union
rep meeting in Terry's room, home for maybe
half hour, then Cottage Inn for a five-hour
shift. I'd like to be running under

a lazy pop-up right now, tracking it into a well-worn
mitt. Here, the breeze shifts papers across my mess
of a desk. Students write about walls, fences, borders,
boundaries tangible and intangible. We read Robert Frost,

listen to Pink Floyd, watch the iconic video where
British kids resist falling into the meat grinder, rip off masks,
overturn chairs, urge their teacher toward a fount of roaring
flames. *There's something about that work, work, work,*

work, work. In 3rd hour, Kyndall, a senior, seems
shaken. She wrote an article for the school newspaper
about a man who was detained by ICE, a father
of two students in our district. He works

in a local restaurant, boasts no criminal record
or citizenship papers. Everyone knows
he's no harm. Kyndall thinks it's too late.
The authorities worked fast. The government,

efficient. He's been sent to a detention center
in Louisiana. Kyndall calls it a giant holding cell,
a cargo-cage for people stickered for shipping.
The President wants a wall. The poet says, *something*

there is that doesn't love a wall. The President wants
a big beautiful wall. *It'll happen,* he says, *believe me.*
Pink Floyd says *we don't need no education.* The softball
players field grounders. At the union meeting we'll talk

about supporting next month's bond so we can repair
infrastructure. So many of our buildings are crumbling.
So many of our students are crumbling. Zach writes about
his girlfriend of two years, how she turned the wall

inside him into *a picket fence anyone could jump over.*
Dylan writes about her best friend, how she might be
too open to believing bruises are beautiful. *Maybe,* Erin
says, *the way she loves you isn't the same way*

she'll act when she's in romantic love. Nick thinks
no one in the world cares a damn about him. One
teacher will suggest we've seen a dramatic uptick
in students struggling with mental health. The rest

of us will nod. The duct tape holding
together the tailgate of my car needs
to be refreshed. Nathaniel concocts
a poster to ask a girl to prom. It features

end-line rhyme.

To the driver fired for forging tips on credit card receipts

I understand why. I too have
admired a spacious house
with expensive porch lights bathing

the lawn and a pair of Lexi hibernating
in the well-tended garage (that includes
a high-powered snowblower and tricked-

out kayak) and peered at the receipt where
the tip line says two bucks or, worse,
hunkers mute. I too have formulated

the equation: zero dollars times twenty-
five minutes for this delivery equals
late fee for my next unpaid property

tax. I too have considered the alchemy
that transforms a 1 into a 4, a 3 into an 8,
but here's the thing—you got caught.

The manager had no choice but to remove
the magnetized sign from your roof. Now
you're gone, and I may never see you again,

though I suspect at some point your sub-compact
will zoom past wearing a hat from a different
establishment and I'll wave, but you won't

see me, or if you do, you'll forget you taught
me how to save time by taking Fifth Avenue
all the way down to Hill, instead of turning

left on Packard, or where to park if I have
a delivery on State when the football traffic
snakes from The Big House to the end

of the known universe. I know you'll be
driving again somewhere. It seemed like
a holographic map would appear in front

of your face and you'd describe the route
I needed to deliver the triple, first take Huron
to the hospital, then out to the condo on Geddes,

then cut across Oxford into The Spaghetti
Bowl to finish with the house on Heather. I'm
pretty sure, on occasion, you even passed up

larger tips just so the map in your mind
would make a kind of spiritual Fibonacci
sequence, a DNA helix revealing the quickest

genetic code for any pilgrimage through
the city. I like to believe this is why you
stole. You live for symmetry and something's

off when the person in the million-dollar
mansion stunts miserly. You were just
trying to balance the community,

make the veins of our civic body flow
more fluidly. You knew what each
delivery should have been worth.

You were a kind of do-it-yourself—
and for your own personal financial
gain—Robin Hood, pissed off and not

merry, driving a dented Chevy
through Sherwood Court. I can't
agree you give all us drivers a bad

name. I just deliver more slowly now
since my shortcut mastery remains
fragmentary. What I do know, I share

with the new drivers. It's your voice
I'm speaking with when I say, *hey,*
let me show you a trick.

Garbage day

Not the kind
where you haul
the bin to the curb.

Just a trash
trash, trashity-
trash, negative
seventy-six
dollars in my bank
account three-hour
morning stuffed
with hectoring juniors
to abandon their phones
at the front of the room,
sequester calculators
beneath their desks,
and refrain from thinking
about sex during the multi-
million-dollar mind-murkifying
mud-mess otherwise known
as the ACT.

Then a lunchtime sophomore
giving a half-assed missed class
make-up speech about videogame
theme music that fails to include
a single actual example of videogame
theme music, followed by yet another
staff meeting devoted to genuflecting
toward the two-headed deity of district-
wide common assessment and uploading
data, and my shift hasn't started well either.

After blowing out a tire on the highway
and then blowing two hundred bucks
for two new ones, my car, in lieu

of purring gratitude, offers instead
a whining growl as if it devoured
a sour ball-bearing sandwich
and I'm in free-fall denial
that this dying-porpoise wail
portends any further outlays
for repairs and my first three
runs are nothing worth celebrating,
a two-dollar tip, a dollar-sixty-six,
a stiff, and when I pull up
to the high-rent high-rise,
I'm surprised at the enthusiasm
of the customer when I call and say,

*Hi, this is Jeff from Cottage Inn, how
you doing?*

I'm fantastic, he says,
really, really terrific,
and every octave
in his voice sings
he means it and he
promises to be down
in the lobby in less
than a minute so I scuttle
from my car to meet him
and he's wearing an off-
white T-shirt featuring
a blood-red illustration
of the Rosetta Stone
or some other ancient
document hand-carved
in cuneiform, and he smiles
like a construction zone
floodlight and tips four
dollars and nineteen
cents on a fifteen-dollars-
and-eighty-one-cents bill
and says, *I just got a job.*

Theoretically, I understand
that's good news, but in practice,
with three of them and a still-
negative account balance,
it's difficult to muster much
positive affirmation.

Nonetheless, I fake it
and ask for more particulars.

We establish amidst a rush
of bubbly gushes he'll be a tour
guide at the science museum
and, sure, that sounds awesome,
then he adds,

You're the first person I told this to.

What, I wonder, is the electric
current of such an assertion?

Did the man startle himself
blurting his good fortune
to a stranger? Are we both
embarrassed that I, dude
pulling $5.25 an hour plus tips,
am the person he chose to favor
with his bliss?

Perhaps to cover the awkwardness
of his vulnerability, or maybe just
to demonstrate my own tomfoolery,
I reach for my most pretentious vocabulary:
*Well, I'm honored to be the recipient of such
glad tidings.* He looks at me like maybe
he made a mistake trusting me with his joy.

He didn't.

For, suddenly, I am joyful too.

I am not just the conveyor of pies and breadsticks.

I am the sounding board for somebody's moment.

I am the human ear that heard a human mouth cascade
    with light.

Take that, future drone
who will one day soon

drop
pies

from
the sky.

For the 3 a.m. road warriors

This is for drivers
with lit-up signs crowning
their automobile roofs.

For those who circle the block

and search

                and circle
and search

                and circle

and search

          for a place to park

          and burn the blink
          out the hazard light.

For those who wait on
the apartment doorstep
hoping for the starstruck luck
of a door opening on the first knock.

For tucking a pen behind
your ear and never forgetting
to ask the customer,
you want your receipt?

For dead-weary eyes
peering at stop signs;
for stomachs buffeted
by speed bumps and potholes;
for legs heavy with snowbank
and staircase.

This is for those who stuff dollars
in their pockets and fish out
change with one ungloved finger
and check the board, hoping
for one last run before it's time
to clock out.

Another school year, another email

says a student has died. It happened downtown.
Believed to be suicide. I knew him. He kept his hair
military, bounced on his toes through the hallway.
Wielded a tennis racket and a big laugh when willing.
I think of him mostly as quiet, chin cocked slightly upward,
eyebrows knitted, thinking. He owned the stage one year
in the poetry slam, made a whole auditorium chortle
at his story of catching his thumb in a car door. He wanted
to be in love.

I wanted him to be in love too. I want all my students to be
in love, so deep and viscous they can't focus in class and my words
sound like trucks backing up, beeping through their bliss. Choose
the bliss. Choose it over anything else I try to teach you. I await
now the next email, letting me know funeral arrangements.
I will go if I can. It will be terrible. A boy, too young not to be
able to engage in more screw-ups. I will say to his mother, he
was a great kid. I will say to my students—brand new, they don't
even know me yet—choose bliss. Nothing else I say is important.
Choose bliss.

Acknowledgments

Thanks to the good people at the *Nashville Review* who originally published the poem "The manager talks about getting engaged."

Much love to the crew at Cottage Inn on Packard who made the difficult nights bearable, especially Patrick and Justin, awesome managers with style and heart.

Thanks too to all my colleagues on C-3 who put up with my slogging up the stairs thirty seconds before the bell (or, sometimes, after it) and wish me the worthiest of all days every single worthy day. And to Maria Montri, especially, for unlocking the door so my students aren't stranded in the hallway without me.

Thanks to the Principal, also with style and heart, Tracey Lowder, who sat me down in his office for an evaluation meeting in the midst of this wild year and told me, *I just want you to be you, except moreso,* which was the exact thing I needed to hear.

I see you, James Giacalone. I see you, Don Packard and Amy Vail (who ain't on C-3, but, you know, she still kinda is).

Thanks to pre-readers of some of these poems: Leslie Handyside, Jessie Hieber, Kyndall Flowers, and whoever else I'm forgetting.

Thanks to Annie, Polly, Kristina, Carrie, and everyone else at Wayne State who believed in and contributed to this project.

Thanks, of course, Karen, Sam, and Julius. Every moment I'm not with the fam is a moment I wish I had back.

Thanks to all teachers and pizza deliverers everywhere just trying to get home safe.

About the Author

JEFF KASS teaches tenth-grade English and creative writing at Pioneer High School in Ann Arbor, Michigan. He is the founder of the literary arts program at Ann Arbor's teen center, the Neutral Zone, where he was program director for twenty years. He is also the author of the award-winning short story collection *Knuckleheads*, the poetry collection *My Beautiful Hook-Nosed Beauty Queen Strut Wave*, and the thriller *Takedown*. He lives in Ann Arbor with the author Karen Smyte and their children, Sam and Julius.